Animal Mandala Coloring Book

This book belongs to:

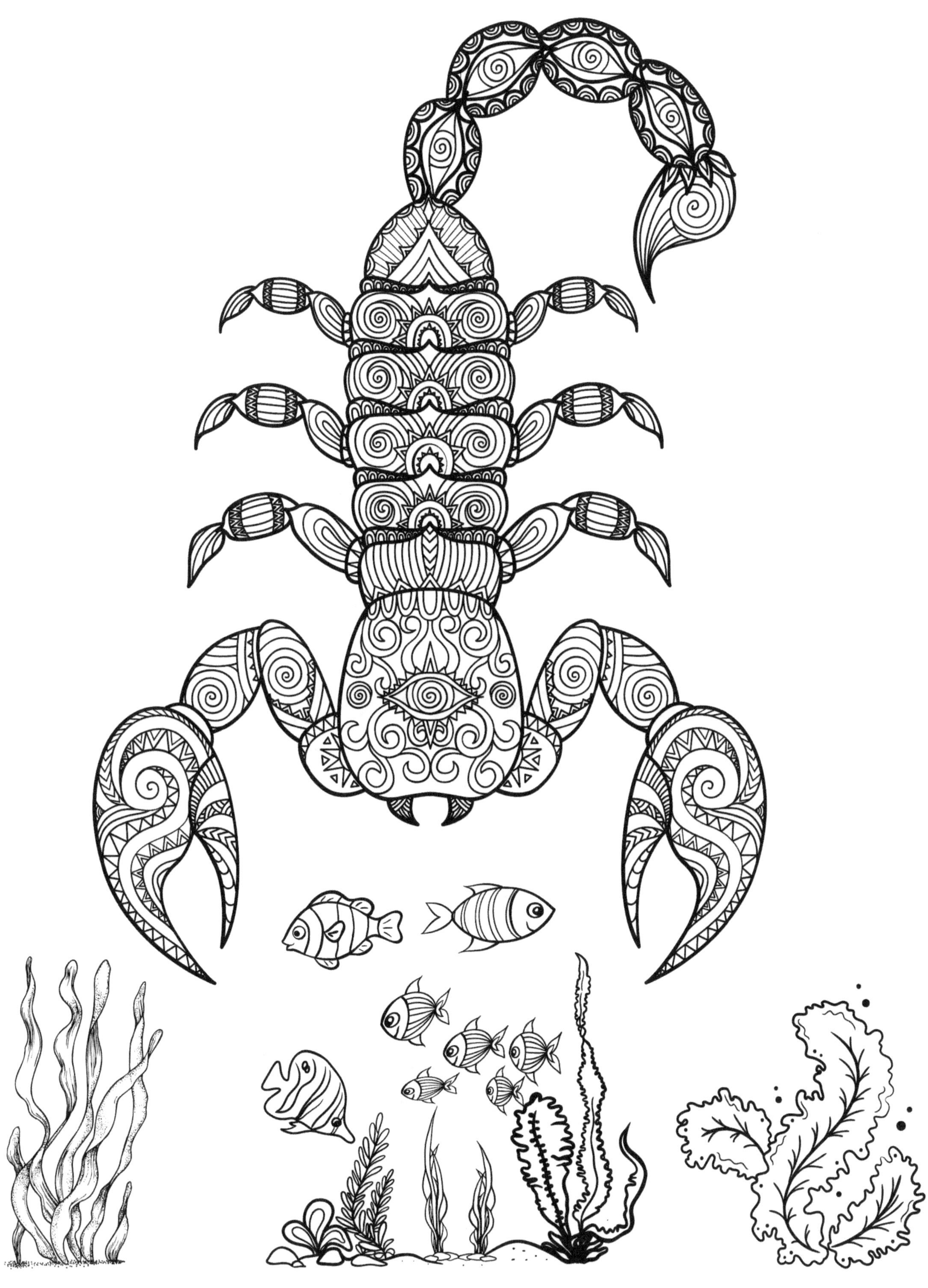

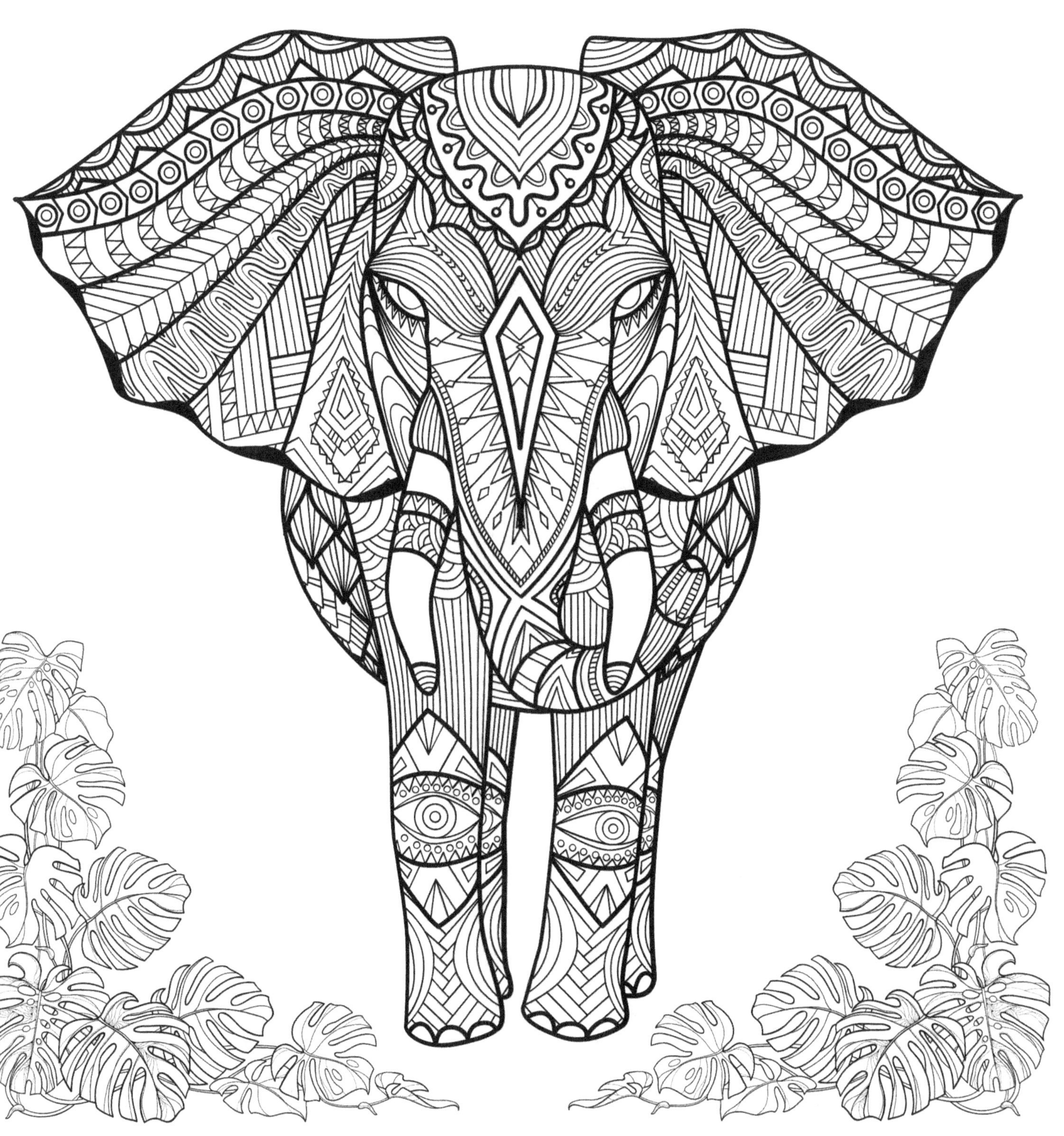

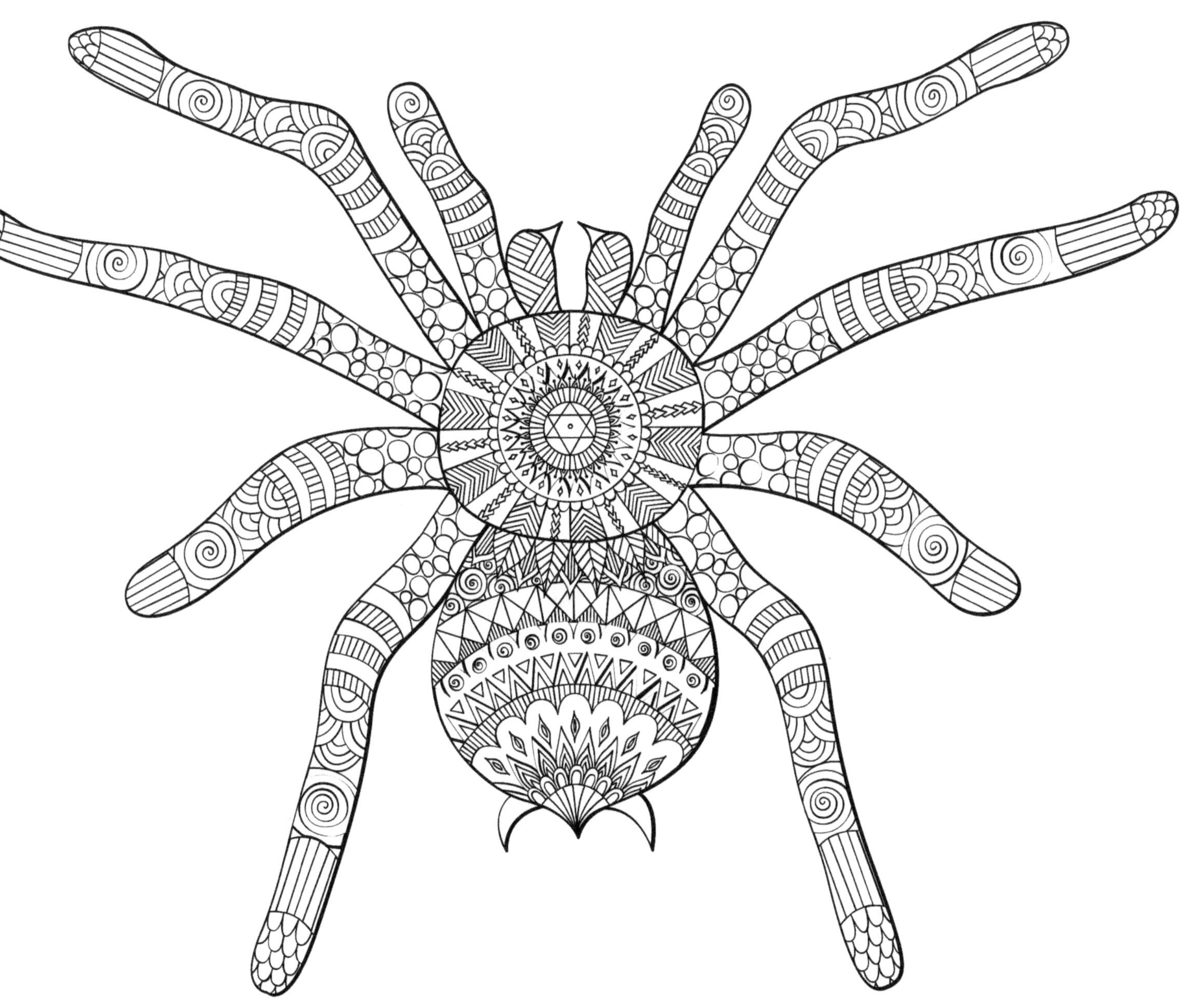

Thank You

Discover more titles at: winmaxpublishers.com

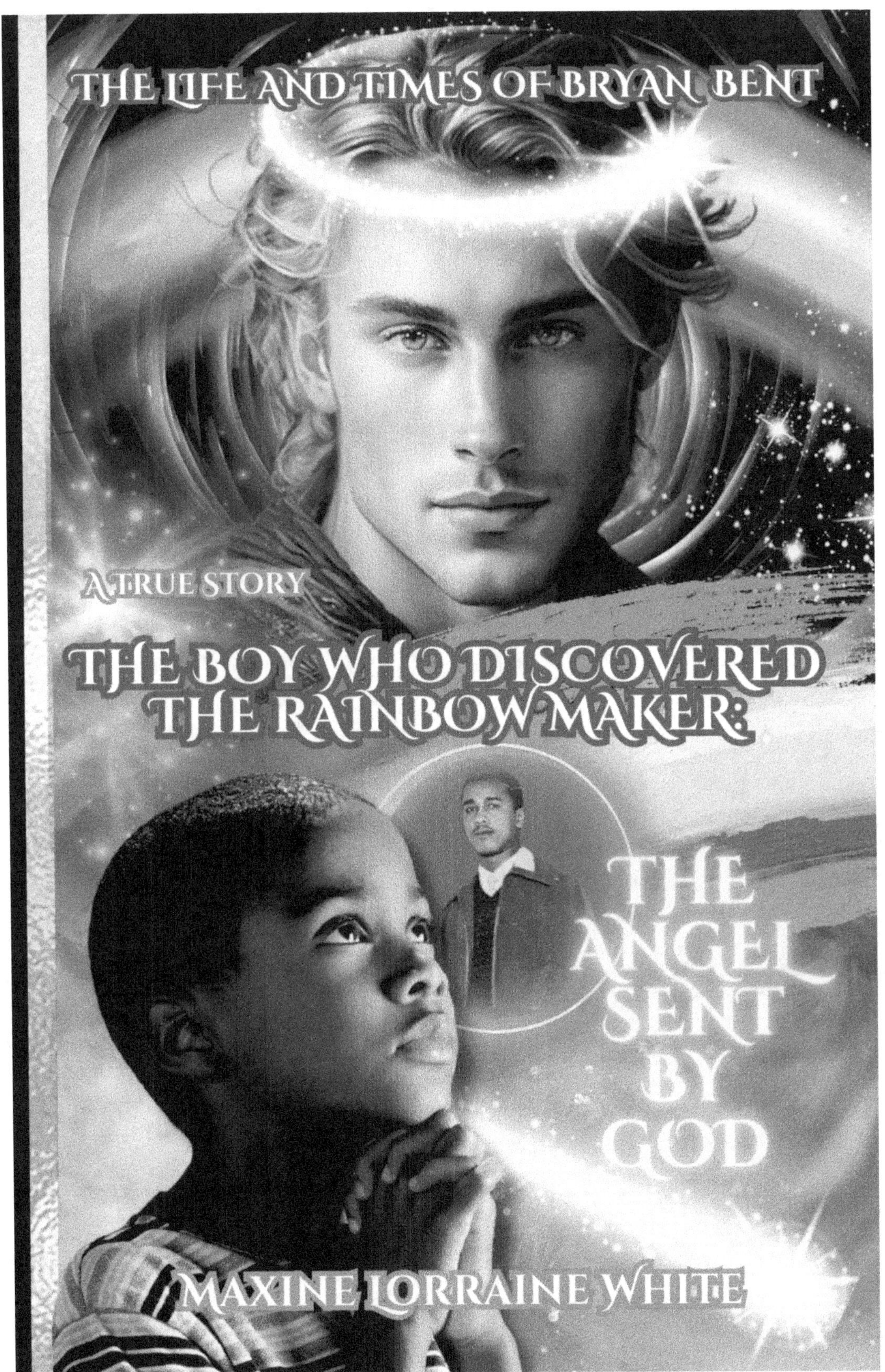

A novel with colourful illustrations

About an angel sent by God to show how rainbows are made, to a little boy in Jamaica over 70 years ago...